BE SAFE AND MIGHTY

BE SAFE AND MIGHTY

BY ALMEASE BYRD, MSW

ALMEASE BYRD
Be Safe and Mighty
Copyright © 2020 by Almease Byrd

Library of Congress Cataloging-in-Publication Data
Name: Byrd, Almease, author.
Registration Number: TXu 2-179-789

First edition

ISBN: 978-0-578-74687-6

Written by Almease Byrd
Illustrated by Zeeshan Saeed
Book Design by Laura Wrubleski
Edited by Lisa of Tangostales
Publishing Support from TSPA The Self Publishing Agency Inc.

To my glorious children – James, Jasten, and Leena.

To the remarkable children I've served in the Los Angeles Unified School District and my fellow school social workers, who tirelessly work to ensure the safety and well-being of our students.

To my champion teachers, administrators, and LAUSD School Mental Health personnel, who relentlessly create safe schools for our students to learn, grow, and develop.

What does it mean
to be safe?

Being safe means staying away from dangerous places, people, or things.

COMPANY NAME

eing safe means
eeping your eyes
nd ears open to what
s happening
round you.

Calm
Lonely
Scared
Excited
Jealous

Angry

Happy

Sad

Being safe means naming and understanding your feelings.

Proud

Surprised

Being safe means telling an adult you trust about things that make you feel uncomfortable.

Being safe means knowing your rights.

Being safe means helping others by treating them with respect and kindness.

Being safe means
stopping, slowing down,
and thinking about
your choices.

Being safe means being careful about what you see and post on social media or the Internet.

Being safe means loving yourself.

Loving your face, hair, and body.

Loving to learn new things.

Loving to eat healthy foods and exercise.

Loving to brush your teeth and keep clean.

Loving to pray and be grateful.

How will you be safe?

Honor and praise to our
Lord and Savior, Jesus Christ.

Blessings and praise to my loving husband,
Richard, for making this all possible.

Extended gratitude to the best teacher
I know — Theresa Brissett-Claxton.

Love and grace to my parents, (Groupship),
Kia Davis, family, and close friends for their
unwavering love and encouragement.

READER'S REFLECTION

☑ Find a setting that is most safe and secure for children while reading and discussing the content of this book.

☑ Read the text of this book with enthusiasm and earnest expression to best nurture their minds and interests.

☑ Ask open-ended questions along the way, and invite children to share what they see happening in the illustrations.

To empower children with knowledge and action-steps that will prepare them to exercise safe choices in their homes, schools, and community environments, reflect on the following before reading this book:

☑ Probe discussions that relate to their life experiences, while validating their response, by actively listening, asking clarifying questions, and providing gentle feedback.

☑ Have fun and openly explore the subject so that children are eager to continue safety conversations with family and peers.

CONVERSATION STARTERS

1. What do you know about being safe?

2. Give me an example of a time when you had to make a safe choice.

3. Tell me more about how to be safe while playing with friends.

4. How do you feel when you are safe? How do you feel when you are unsafe?

5. Who do you trust to help keep you safe?

6. How do you plan to protect yourself from hurtful words?

The explanations of safety in this book are written for you to have restorative, critical conversations about the very thoughts, feelings, and choices essential for preparing a child to put safety first. Consider using these conversation starters while reading this book to young learners:

7 How can you be most helpful when you see someone else being unsafe?

8 If you could create a super safe community, what would it look like? Draw a picture.

9 Let's name and discuss the safety rules at home, school, and in your community.

10 What more do you want to know about being safe?